CW00828035

いうか、どの一枚にも凛々と鳴っているものがあった。紛れもない本当の登山家が、本当の穂高撮影者がここには居る、そんな思いであった。

　併し、こうした私の感動は、そう的外れではないであろうと思う。と言うのは、ここ三十年ほど、一番気候のいい時であるにしても、毎年一回、穂高には登り続けているからである。穂高という山が好きなことにかけては、人後におちない。穂高だけが好きなのであり、穂高以外の山は知らない。穂高オンリーである。四十八歳から七十代の後半まで穂高詣でを続けている。

　その穂高の最もきびしい時期に、氏は毎年のように穂高に登り続け、遭難も経験されながら、その穂高のきびしさも、優しさも、美しさも、穂高のすべてをカメラに収め続けて来られているのである。氏の本当の山への愛情に対し、お仕事の真剣さに対して、心から敬意を表し、この小文の筆を擱くことにする。

……………………作家

INTRODUCTION

Yasushi Inoue

I was shown the photographs of Hodaka taken by Mr. Mizukoshi when his photographs of mountain landscape taken over the last twenty years were being compiled into a book. They comprised of only monochromes. When I first saw them, all I could say was, "They're fantastic." Being a layman, I could not professionally tell you if they were good or not, however, owing to them being monochrome I truly thought Mizukoshi's Hodaka was wonderful. Whether the naked beauty of Hodaka was captured or whether Hodaka itself was captured, I could not take my eyes off them. Hodaka in winter is harsh and beautiful as well as serene.

To take a close look at 10–20 photographs, I laid out a gigantic batch of them on top of the table. While looking at one after another, I felt this was something that you should not thumb through and even now the impact I got from seeing Hodaka lingers with me. Could it be its severe harshness or could it be its austere beauty? You could feel a pierce ringing in each picture. I thought without

a doubt this is a true mountaineer; this is a true Hodaka photographer.

Being deeply impressed I do not think my 6th sense is mistaken. For these twenty years or so

when the weather is fine I have climbed Hodaka every year. My fondness for this mountain Hodaka

is second to none. I am in love with Hodaka and I know of no other mountain. I am devoted myself

to Hodaka. Since 48 years old up to my late 70's I have continued on my pilgrimage to Hodaka.

He has climbed Hodaka every year during the bleakest season. While experiencing disasters,

he has captured the austerity, the superbness and the beauty of Hodaka on camera. I write these

words to express my deepest respects to his genuine love for mountains and his dedication to his work.

···························Novelist

5

エディトリアル・ディレクター：赤平覚三
Editorial Director: **Kakuzo Akahira**

ブック・デザイン：鈴木一誌
Book Design: **Hitoshi Suzuki**

目次
Contents

風を見る
A View toward the Wind

カールの底から
Rim of the Basin

雪煙上る
Snow's Breath

地吹雪
Snow Desert

季節風
Rivers of Wind

西穂高西面
West Hodaka: Winter Facade

エビノシッポ I
Lobster Tail I (Silver Thaw)

エビノシッポ II
Lobster Tail II (Silver Thaw)

雪解け
Melting Snow

雪壁
Snow Wall

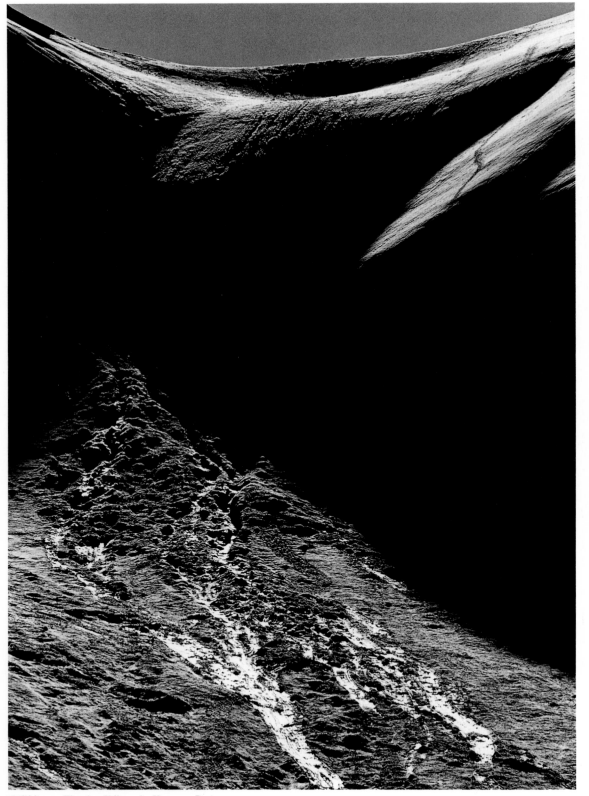

涸沢カール　Waterless Valley : the Karesawa Basin

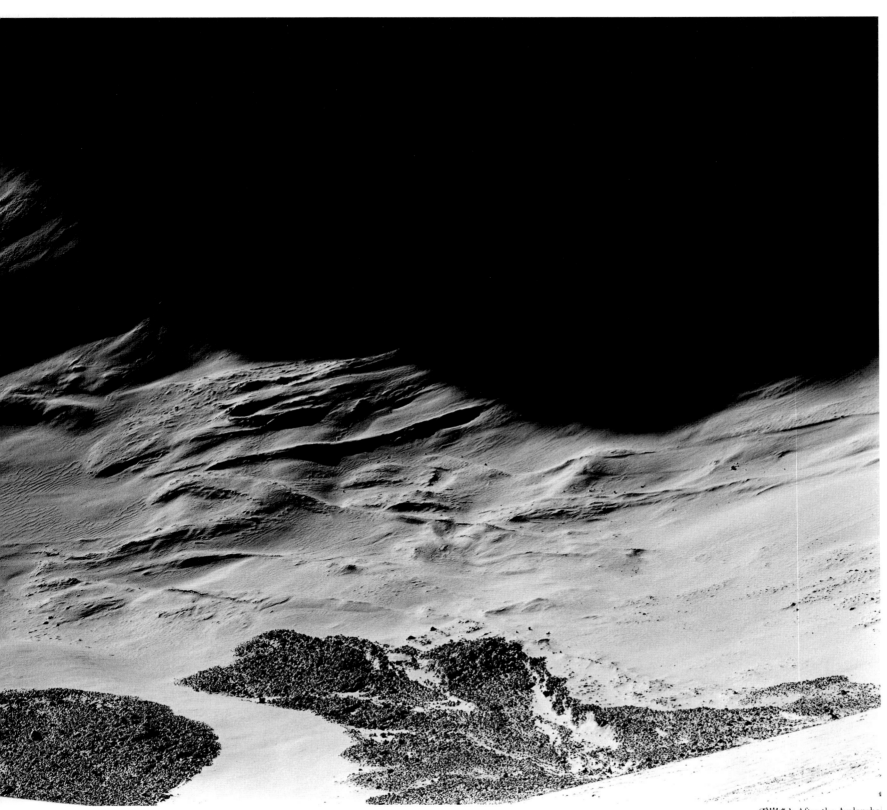

雪崩あと After the Avalanche

北穂高から槍ヶ岳
View from North Hodaka : Yarigadake

北穂高北壁
North Wall of Kita-Hodaka

冬の槍ヶ岳
Yarigadake Peak

明神岳主峰
Myojindake Peak

ジャンダルム飛騨尾根
The Hidaone Gendarme

春の奥穂高岳
Spring Summit : Oku-Hodaka

初雪の奥穂高岳
Winter Sign: First Snowfall on Oku-Hodaka

午後のジャンダルム
The Sentinel Unmasked: Gendarme at Midday

前穂高岳
Mae-Hodaka Peak

滝谷の冬
Takidani in Winter

槍平から滝谷を望む
View from Yaridaira: Takidani in Clouds

厳冬の穂高稜線
Winter Purgatory: the Hodaka Ridge

奥穂高
Mountain Depths : Oku-Hodaka

雪崩
Avalanche

北尾根から山頂を望む
Toward the Summit from Kitaone

涸沢岳
The Peak of Karesawa

二月の西穂高
The Face of February : West Hodaka

残照の奥穂高岳
Lingering Pleasure : Oku-Hodaka at Twilight

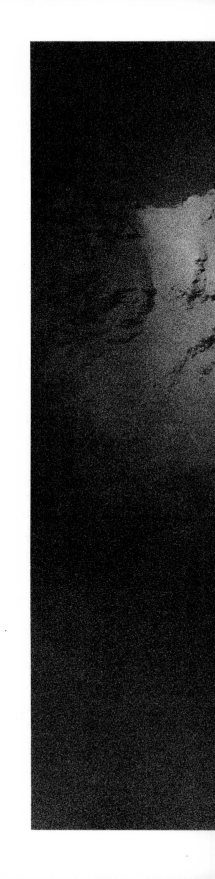

冬の前穂高山頂より
Wintry Gaze from the Summit of Mae-Hodaka

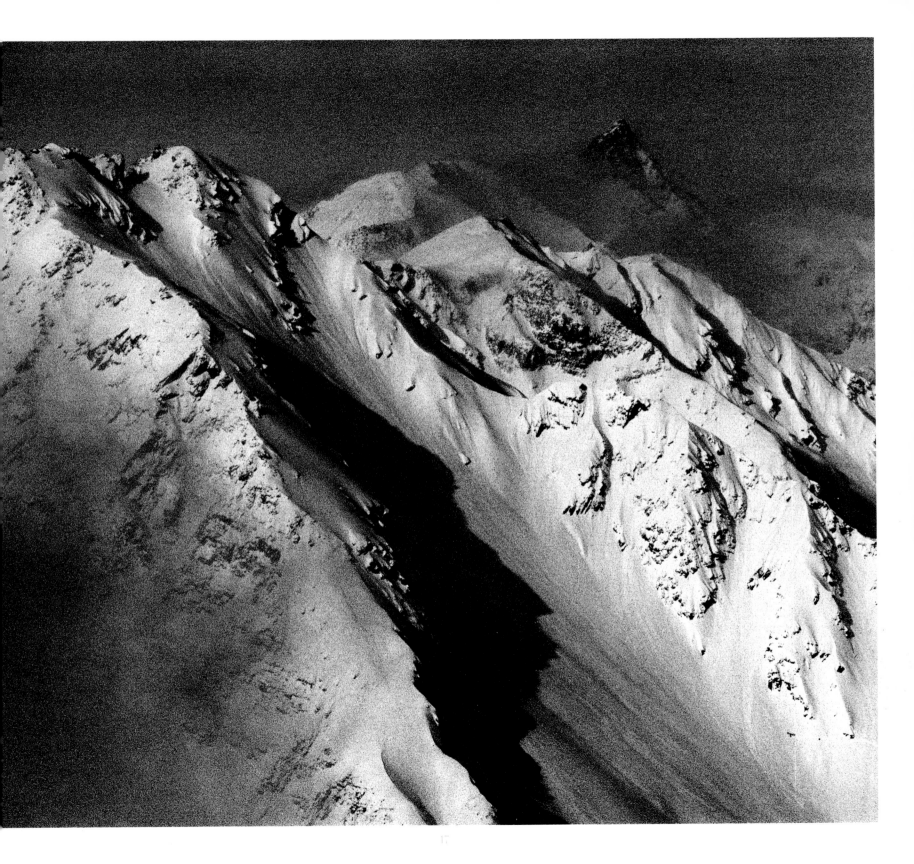

雪の梓川
Archipelago of Snow : the Azusa River

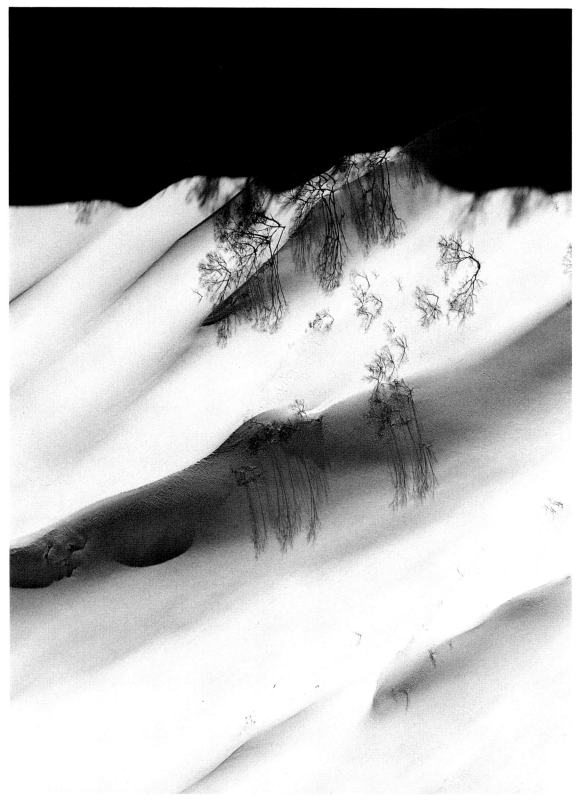

ダケカンバの尾根
Birches at One

冬の上高地
Kamikochi in Winter

氷
Ice Echoes

朝の梓川
The Azusa River Dawn

明神にて
Memories of Myojin

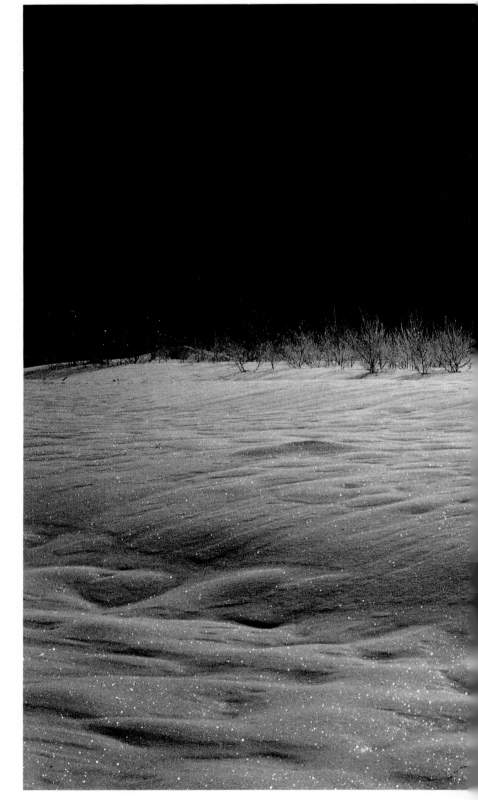

凍結した梓川
The Azusa River Frozen

五月のケショウヤナギ
May Willows

冬の徳合峠
Winter Heights: The Tokugou Pass

豪雨の梓川
Cloudburst on the Azusa River

秋の空
Fall Sky

秋の大正池
Peering into a Dream: Fall at the Taisho Pond

霧氷
Silver Thaw

影のパターンⅠ Shades of Form Ⅰ

影のパターン III
Shades of Form III

吹雪のあと
Wind Tracings of Snow

涸沢
Karesawa

カールの底
Depth of the Basin

新雪のカール
The Basin in Fresh Snow

冬が来る
Premonition : Winter's First Cry

滝谷二尾根
Escarpment: Nione at Takidani

明神2263峰
Myojin Peak 2263

初冬のキレット
Early Winter Fissure

滝谷にて
At Takidani

雪煙舞う
Dancing on the Wind

雪稜
Snow Shoulder

雪庇
Snow Eaves

冬の焼岳
Yakidake in Winter

雪の造型
Traces in Snow

奥穂高岳
Oku-Hodaka Peak

北穂高から前穂高岳
The Peak Mae-Hodaka Viewed from North Hodaka

屏風岩
Byobuiwa

凍結した滝谷
Takidani in the Ice

厳冬の西穂高岳
Deep Winter at West Hodaka

三月の穂高連峰
Spring Ridge : The Hodaka Range in March

蝶ヶ岳を望む
Metamorphosis: A Vision of Chogatake

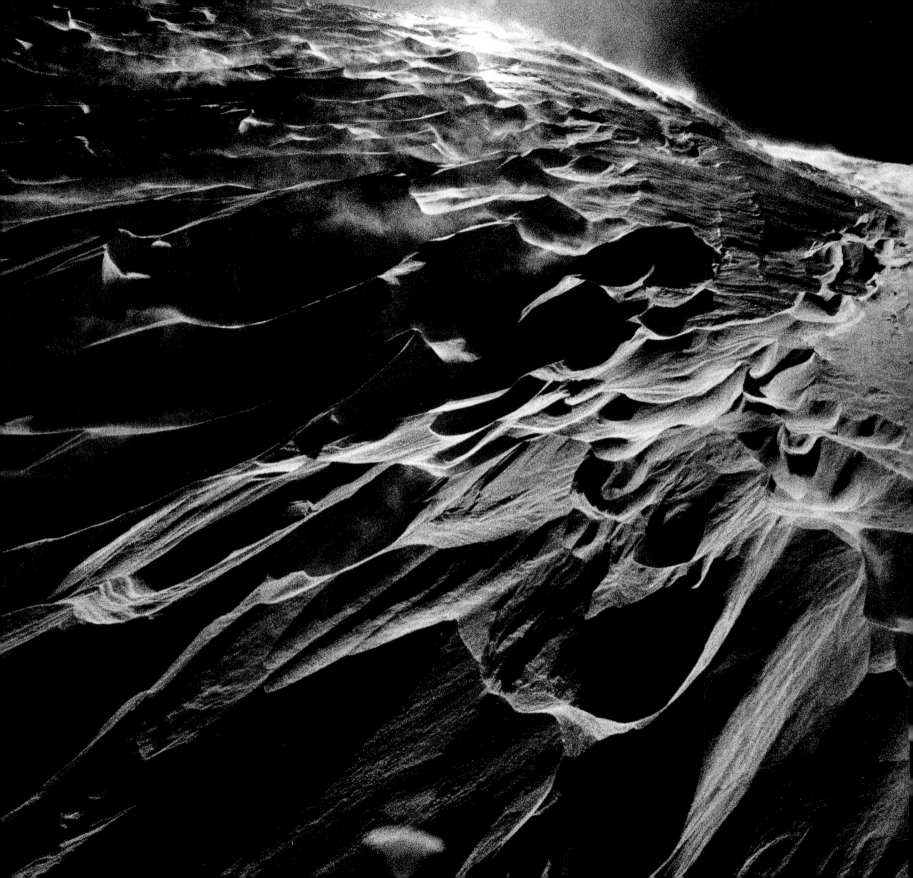

雪煙
Wind-Climbing Snow

私が高等学校に入学した年の夏、烏帽子岳から槍ヶ岳に縦走をした。野口五郎岳から鷲羽、双六と日程が進むにしたがい、今まで見たこともない険しい峰々が、黒々としたボリュウムある岩肌に残雪を抱きながら毎日少しずつ近づいてくる。それが私が初めて接した穂高連峰の姿であった。その時受けた深い感動が機縁となって、その後30年今日まで穂高にすっかり心を奪われた私は、この山とともに人生を歩むようなこととなる。

穂高は私の青春とともにあった山である。穂高を慕い、心を通わさんと、年に200日以上も穂高周辺をうろついていた時期もあった。だれでも10年20年一つの山とつきあっていると、どうしてもぬぐいさることのできないいくつかの思いが生まれてくるものである。

私の中にもそんな穂高への思いなり、想い出がいくつもある、それを二、三ひろってみたい。

◉

もうあれから10年以上もたってしまった。日本の経済が高度成長期にあり、何か毎日がお祭り騒ぎにあるような感じで、人びとの価値観もどんどんと変わっていくような時であった。そんな社会の波に違和感を抱く若者が山にも入ってきた。当時ヒッピーなどと言われていた人たちである。

穂高の涸沢にもそんな人たちが何人か、2ヵ月も3ヵ月も下山することもなく、岩登りなどをしてテントで暮していた。当時は食糧やアルコールも友人からもらったり拾ったりして不自由することはなかった。

私も6月下旬に2、3日分の食糧を持って涸沢に入山し、そのまま彼らとともにひと夏過ごした。そんな浮世離れした生活をしていても、山の季節は巡ってゆく。9月も半ばを過ぎると朝夕の冷え込みは厳しく、夏の装備しか持ちあわせのない我々には辛くなってきた。一人去り、二人去り、涸沢にあふれていたテントも寂しくなってくる。

明日は山を下ると決めた朝、友人二人と最後の登攀に滝谷に向かった。それ程むずかしくないルートであったが、途中私が写真など撮っていたりして、北穂の頂上に帰りついた時はとっくに落日は笠ヶ岳に沈んでいた。

蝶ヶ岳から昇った月も前穂に高くかかり、谷は暗く静かに夜のとばりにつつまれていた。

こんな時刻に山をうろついている人間は、我々三人だけだった。満月に近い月光は思いのほか強く、山の輪郭をはっきりと浮きたたせ、岩壁やすっかりやせ細った残雪を青白く照らしだしていた。凜とした空気があたりを包み、なぜか我々も異常な精神状態に包まれ山頂を去り難く、歌など歌って、1時間もたたずんでいた。

この時見た月光に照らされた穂高ほど、山が美しいと思ったことはなかった。

この3ヵ月間、昨日は前穂東壁、今日はジャンダルムと穂高のど真中でテントを張り毎日穂高と顔を合わせていたが、こんな夢のように美しい穂高は初めてだった。

知り尽くしていると思っていた山にも、まだまだ想像もできない表情がある。

穂高に、山は我々がこんなものだと考えているよりもはるかに大きな存在であることを教わった。

二人の友人は、一人はヨーロッパアルプスに行ったまま帰らず、一人は山から遠ざかり東京の巷に消えてしまった。

あの時、これは我々だけの穂高だ、我々だけの王国だと叫んだ穂高は、とうとう私一人

わが内なる穂高

水越武

の穂高になってしまった。

◉

　この時期は5月のゴールデンウィークの、山好きの人間なら誰でも自分の山行計画をたてる時期だった。

　友人と二人、彼は飛騨側から滝谷の4尾根を登り、私は上高地から涸沢へとゆっくり撮影しながら、奥穂高の山小屋で落ち合う約束をした。そしていつも暖かく迎えてくれる穂高岳山荘でゆっくり酒でも飲もうと話しあっていた。

　約束の前日には、私は穂高岳山荘に入った。次の日に快晴となり、泊り合わせた二人の若い男と一緒に奥穂高に登った。

　奥穂高の頂上はカメラマンにとって実にありがたい天国のようなところである。360度の展望があり、前穂、北穂、ジャンダルムとそれぞれ個性的な立派な姿をしている。

　今日は一日、太陽の位置によって次々とその姿を変えていく山を楽しむのだ、と私は奥穂高の山頂にどっしりと腰を落ちつけた。一緒に登ってきた二人は、前穂から岳沢に下るべく雪稜になった吊尾根をたどり始めた。時間にして10分、距離にして100メートルも行かない私の目の前で、その内の一人が足をすべらせ、すっと音もなく消えていった。当時は電話も無線も山にはなかった時代である。私はただその遭難を早く知らせるために、涸沢までグリセードでとばし、3時間ほどで木村小屋に着いたことを覚えている。

　次の日から遭難救助活動が始まった。私は酒を飲む約束をした友人のことなどすっかり忘れて、頼まれるままその手伝いをしていた。遭難者を収容し、一段落したので、その時汚れた靴下などを梓川で洗い、河原の石の上に乾していた時であった、知人から私の友人の遭難を聞いたのは。友人は滝谷の4尾根で滑落、もう遺体は新穂高におろされ、茶毘にふされた後であった。それを聞くと私はそのまま、この季節特有の暗いガスにまかれている穂高を前に坐り込んでしまった。考えてみれば友人と約束した日から3日も過ぎている。

　この時の深い悲しみと怒り、これは何に対してだったのか、友人に対してだったのか、また名も知らなかった遭難者に対してだったのか、それとも穂高に対してか、何かむしょうに腹が立ち、大きな声でわめき叫びたいような気持だった。

　今考えてみると、この怒りは私自身に対してだったのにちがいない、自分で自分を許せなく腹がたったのであろう。この記憶は今だに私の心の中で尾を引いている。

　こんな私の情念の世界にも、穂高と切り離せない絆がある。

◉

　それは記録的な豪雪にみまわれた1970年の冬山であった。日本海に近い剣岳では連日異常な降雪があり、自力で脱出できないパーティが続出し、大量遭難をだしたことで記憶にある人も多いと思う。

　私は年の暮れまでに横尾尾根から南岳を単独で往復、新年早々に入山してくる友人のパーティを迎えて畳岩尾根から奥穂高を登攀する二つの山行計画をたてた。

　クリスマスイヴに40キロを超える荷を背に沢渡をスタート、先行パーティがあってラッセルの必要もなく、夕方には徳沢園に着いた。次の日も朝から雪がちらついていたが、本谷からカンバ尾根にとりつき、2,000メートル近くで小さな雪洞をほってビバーク、この日はひと晩中ゴーゴーと鳴る風の音が耳について、まんじりともしないで一夜を明かした。

明るくなっても風も雪も止まないが出発する。森林限界を越え、横尾尾根に出てから横なぐりの風雪が強く行動をストップし、吹きだまりに時間をかけて雪洞を作った。呼吸も困難を感じるような風雪から、雪洞の中に入ると外の世界が嘘のようだ。雪で棚を作りローソクを立てると、まわりの雪に光が反射して驚くほど明るくなる。外のうなるような風の音もとどいてはこない。窮屈な手袋を脱いでも指先はこごえない。何者にも邪魔されない一人だけの空間に心からほっとする。

　晴れれば目の前に白く輝く北穂高を楽しみに、1日、2日と雪洞の中で暮らす。しかし3日もすると時間の観念が薄れてくる。そしてあれ程天国だと感じた雪洞の中で、たった一人だけで話す相手もいない寂しさが苦になってくる。快適だと思っていた雪洞も、床に凹凸ができたり、天井が下がってきて生活環境を悪化させる。春とちがってこの季節の雪はやわらかく、どうしてもゆがみが出てきてしまう。

　雪洞で4日目の朝を迎えても、冬型の気圧配置は変わらず、ますます風雪は強まるばかりである。あれほどかたい決心をして一人重い荷物を背に、一歩一歩ワカンでラッセルをして登ってきたのに、一枚のシャッターもきることなく吹雪の中を下山してしまった。

　新しい年に気をとり直し、友人と上高地で合流、岳沢から畳岩尾根にむかった。何日も続いた雪で雪崩の危険を感じながらも、強引にとりつき高度をかせぐ。雪の止むのを待って行動していたのでは、いつまでたっても動きがとれないということもあって、降雪の中を登って行った。

　とりついてから3日目、今日は稜線に出られるという日、新雪雪崩が我々のパーティを直撃、私は強い衝撃を受け空中に投げ出されたが、ロープにぶらさがるだけで助かった。4名中、2名が流された。いくら大きな声で呼んでも返事はない。吹雪の中では声が雪に吸いとられ、こだまも帰ってこない。どれほど時間がたったであろうか、5分、10分、われわれには長く感じられたが、ほんとうは2、3分であったろう。

　小さな黒点が二つ、白い斜面をゆっくりトラバースしていくのが吹雪をすかして見える。目を疑うとはこんな時にいうのだろう。あれは仲間にちがいない。それから懸垂下降を始めた。その時支点にかけた筈のロープがはずれていて、滑落しそうになるという、我々がどれほど焦っていたかを証明するようなハプニングがあったが、全員命だけは無事で河童橋に立つことができた。

　大正池まできて、我々が悪戦苦闘した尾根を探そうと振り返ったが、雪に白く煙っていてとうとう見つけることができなかった。

　半月という決して短かくはない日々、ついに穂高は一度もピークを見せることなく、私はレンズを向けることもできずに穂高を後にした。

　この時、軽度の顔面凍傷を負っていたが、極度に緊張していたので、そんなことはたいして気にもならなかった。

　どんなにあがこうが自然の流れに逆らうことはできない。人間の卑小さを穂高から悟らされた15日間の山行であった。

◉

　穂高には私の小さな初登攀の思い出もある。今日の新しいテクニックを使えば簡単に登れるルートだ。しかしそんなことはどうでもよい。それは私の中で宵の明星のように時間

とともに少しずつ輝きを増してくる。

　春夏秋冬、私は穂高に足繁く通った。自然を見る眼も、その触れ方までも穂高から私は教わった。穂高を登るという行動から人生の大切なものを学んできたように思う。そして私は穂高を巡って自分の夢を育ててきた。

　26歳で写真を始め、穂高の北風がたたきつける岩壁、深いラッセルを強いる雪稜、地吹雪が渦巻く山頂に自分を立たせシャッターを切ってきた。写真を始めて20年、穂高が好きでこの山の魅力だけにひかれて撮影してきたとは言い難い。正直に自分の心をのぞけば、さまざまなものに対する欲望、戦いといった男のドロドロとした業とけっして無縁ではなかった。

　弱い人間である私は、怒りとか自分のコンプレックスをひきずりながら、吹雪の岩稜を死に物狂いてたどっていたことを白状しなければならない。

　きっと私の穂高は、精神的な渇きをいやす水を求めてさまよう旅であったにちがいない。この旅は一生続く終りのない旅だ。そして自分を見つけ出すための人生をかけた旅でもある。

MY HODAKA

Takeshi Mizukoshi

In summer of my first year in high school I traversed from Mt. Eboshi-dake to Mt. Yarigatake. From Mt. Noguchigorodake I wanted to proceed on a daily schedule to Washu and Sugoroku. As I continued on, a rugged peak which I had never seen before whose deep black bulky rocky surface blanketed with snow of yesteryear came closer little by little with each passing day. This was my initial contact with the continuous rambling peaks of Hodaka. Deeply impressed by it at that time, it became my inspiration. Since then up to this day, 30 years later, I have been completely captive by Hodaka and my life has progressed intertwined with it.

Hodaka was the mountain of my youth. Idolizing Hodaka, I have spent over 200 days of a year wondering around its circumference. During 10 to 20 years when one is intimate with one mountain, one has many memories which one can not completely erase from one's mind. I also have sentiments and memories of Hodaka which I would like to expand on and share with you.

◉

It was over ten years ago, which was the period of Japan's high growth when each day was like a festival. It was a time when people's values were changing. Meanwhile, some young people who were misfits in this kind of society retreated to the mountains. They were called hippies then.

There was such a group of hippies at Karesawa in Hodaka. Not coming down from the mountain for several months they climbed the rocks, pitched their tents and lived there. It was a free life without inconveniences where you shared your food and alcohol with friends.

In late June I also went up to Hodaka carrying 2-3 days supply of food and found myself spending the summer with them. Even though living a life free from worldliness, the seasons in the mountains continued to evolve and by the latter half of September the coldness had started to set in the mornings and evenings. Having only summer equipment with us it started to become strenuous. Members of our group left one after another and the once packed tent became lonely.

In the morning we decided to come down from the mountain the next day, two friends and I headed for our last climb to Takidani. It was not so difficult route. After taking pictures along the way the sun had already gone down behind Mt. Kasaga-Dake by the time we returned to the peak of Kita-Hodaka. The moon rising from Mt. Chogatake shone high above Mt. Mae-Hodaka as the dark night fell softly on the valley. There we were, just the three of us, the only humans roaming around the mountains at that time of night. The nearby moonlight of the full moon was very strong. As it clearly traced the outline of the mountains, it casted its bluish white light over the rocky walls and the remaining strips of snow. The air ringing with a piercing coldness enveloped us. Unexplainably we were in an unusual mental state as we walked away from the peak. Singing songs we lingered on for an hour more. I do not think I have ever seen a lovelier mountain than Hodaka basked in moonlight at that time.

During those three months pitching my tent one day at the Mae-Hodaka eastern wall and the other days right in the middle of Gendarme I came face to face with Hodaka everyday. But it was the first time when Hodaka was so beautiful like a dream. Even when I thought I knew all I could about mountains there were still unimaginable facets of her. Though I knew what a mountain was, I clearly discovered a far greater existence at Hodaka then.

As for my two friends, one went to the Alps in Europe and never came back, while the other left the mountains and disappeared into the streets of Tokyo. At that time, it was just our mountain. Finally in the end Hodaka, which we called our kingdom, became the Hodaka of one-mine.

◉

Another instant was during Golden Week in May when all mountain lovers made their plans for the mountains. My friends and I had made a promise to rendezvous at a small mountain lodge in Oku-Hodaka. He was going to climb the fourth ridge of Takidani from the Hida side, while I was going to leisurely take pictures from Kamikochi to Karesawa. Then, we would meet as we always did at Hodaka-Dake Mountain Lodge to enjoy easy-going drinking and talking.

I got to the Hodaka Mountain Lodge the day before the rendezvous. The next day was a fine, clear day and I went climbing with two other young men who happened to be staying at the same lodge. Carrying my camera with me as I walked along summit of Mt. Oku-Hodaka I marveled at the heavenly sight before me. With a 360 view I could see each of the individual fantastic sights of Mt. Mae-Hodaka, Kita-Hodaka and Gendarme where depending on the position of the sun, the scenerey and forms changed during the day. I had a great time watching the mountain change and was completely at ease. The two who were climbing with me began to follow the snow covered Tsuri-One Ridge that was supposed to go down from Mae-Hodaka to Takesawa. About ten minutes later and not even going more than 100 meters, before my eyes one of them slipped and fell disappearing without a sound. In those days there were no telephones or radios in the mountains. To hurry and notify the accident as quickly as possible, I sped on a glissade to Karesawa and reached Kimura Lodge about three hours later. The rescue operations started the next day. Completely forgetting my rendezvous with my friend I stayed on to help doing only what I was told. We evacuated the victim. During a pause, I washed my soiled socks in the Azusa River and dried them on a rock at the river bed. I heard afterwards from an acquaintance that my friend in the accident had slipped and fell down the fourth ridge of Takidani. The corpse had already been brought down to Shin-Hodaka and cremated. Upon hearing that I just flopped down in front of Hodaka that was enshrouded by a dark curtain of gas that was characteristic of the season. Three days had passed since my planned rendezvous with my friend. I was filled with anger and sorrow.

Who or what could I direct this to my friend or the victim whose name I did not even know, or to Hodaka? I had so much rage inside that I was dying to scream at the top of my voice.

Looking back now, this anger was no doubt at myself. It was probably because I was unable to forgive myself. This memory to this day still pulls at my heart. Even in this passion of mine, I can not break away from Hodaka.

◉

In winter in 1970 we were struck by a tremendous snowfall. It had been snowing consecutively for several days at Tsurugidake near the Japan Sea. One after another party could not get out from under the snow storm by themselves and I think many people remember the massive rescue operations of that year.

I had planned two mountain excursions, going back and forth from Yoko-One Ridge to Mt. Minamidake at the end of the year by myself and meeting friends who wanted to go to the mountains at the beginning of the New Year and climb from Tatamiiwa-One Ridge to Oku-Hodaka.

I started off at Christmas to Sawado with over forty kilo. of equipment on my back. As there was a previous party no russeling was needed and I reached Tokusawaen by nightfall. Also, as it had been snowing from the morning the following day, as well, I made a bivouac by digging a small snow shelter close to 2000m lying from this valley to Kanba-One Ridge. With the wind howling in my ear day and night I stayed awake all night until dawn broke at last. Although it became brighter the next day, the wind and snow did not stop and I departed. After crossing over the timberline and leaving Yokoo-One Ridge, the side sweeping wind and snow grew stronger so that I had to stop. It took time against the snowdrift to build a shelter. Because it seemed difficult to breathe on account of the wind and snow when I entered the shelter the outside world seemed many thousands of miles away. Setting up a candle on the shelf I made, the light reflecting from the surrounding snow walls made it amazingly bright. The shelter even shutted out the groaning wind. In addition, when I removed my tight gloves my fingertips did not freeze from the cold. Without any interference I was alone by myself in this space and felt quite relieved.

Looking forward to seeing a white glistening Kita-Hodaka before by eyes if it cleared up, I lived 2-3 days in that snow shelter. By the third day I began to lose a conception of time. The loneliness started to wear on me without having anyone to talk to while sitting alone in the snow shelter I thought was heaven. Bumps developed in the floor which I thought was so comfortable and the ceiling began to sag as the living environment worsened. This snow, different from spring snow, was soft and distortions were unpreventable.

I awoke my fourth morning in the snow shelter. The wind and snow had clearly intensified with no change in the wintry distribution of atmospheric pressure. Despite my strong convictions to climb alone step by step by russeling on snow shoes with a heavy backpack, I came down the mountain in the snow storm without even taking a shot.

Revitalizing my spirit with the New Year, I joined my friends at Kamikochi and headed for our trek from Takesawa to Tatamiiwa-One Ridge. While apprehensive of the dangers of snowslides resulting from the last consecutive days of snowing, we pushed forward toiling towards Kamikochi. We proceeded on waiting for the snow to stop. It seemed no matter how long we waited we would not move. We climbed in the falling snow.

The third day was the cited day we would reach the ridgeline, however, a fresh snow avalanche hit us. Upon receiving the impact I was thrown into the midair. Luckily I was saved by only a hanging rope. Meanwhile two of our four party members were swept away. No matter how loud we shouted, no answer came back. Our voices had been sucked in by the snow in the snow storm and not even an echo could be heard. I wonder how long we waited-5 or 10 minutes? It seemed like eternity but it was probably only 2-3 minutes. Then peering through the whipping snow, we could see two tiny black figures struggling slowly up the slope. We could not believe our eyes. It was them. From there we commenced our steep decline. At that time the rope that was supposed to have been fixed at the fulcrum slipped as we almost fell. Such happenings proved how much in a hurry we were. With all our lives safe we were able to stand on the Kappa-bashi Bridge.

Reaching the Taisho Pond, we turned around looking for the ridge we fought so hard but were unable to find it under the glistening white snow. The half of a month was by no means short days. In the end Hodaka never did show us her peak. So unable to take her photograph I left Hodaka. At this time I had a mild case of frostbite on my face, but due to my extreme tenseness, I did not pay very much attention to it. No matter how hard you try, you can not go against the flow of nature. It was this fifteen day mountain excursion that I realized from Hodaka the smallness of man.

I also have memories of my first small mountain climbing excursions at Hodaka. If I had used today's new techniques, it would have been an easier route. Anyway, it does not matter. Like the evening star inside of me, my love for mountains grew brighter little by little with passing time. I have frequently traversed across Hodaka on foot in spring, summer, fall, and winter. By seeing nature and coming in contact with it through this way, Hodaka has been my teacher. I believe that I have learned the importance of life from climbing Hodaka. My pilgrimages to Hodaka have also nurtured my dreams.

Beginning photographing at 26 years old, I have stood on the summit alone taking photographs of the rocky walls beaten by the north wind of Hodaka, the rugged snow packed down by deep russels and ground snow storms whipping in swirls. Twenty years have passed since I first started photographing and it is difficult to say that because I like Hodaka it was the magnetism of the mountain that solely attracted me to photograph it. With the exception of my passion, it was not totally unrelated to the grim and sweat of a man's lust and fight for various things. I am a weak creature and

I must confess of having insanely pursue to death on jagged rocks in a snow storm while I drag my anger and complexes with me.

My Hodaka which is undoubtedly like a spiritual search for water to quench my thirst, is a lifetime never-ending journey. It is a journey putting my life on the line to find myself.

撮影ノート

●愛しても愛しきれない、登っても登りきれない、写しても写しても撮りきれない穂高という印象の強い山行であった。

●山は、季節により、気象により、時刻によってその表情を刻々と変幻させる。

●山と対処するには35ミリの小型カメラが有利であるという私なりの考え方から、本書に収録した90％以上は35ミリカメラを利用したものである。

●20年間という長期にわたっての撮影であったため、多様なカメラ、フィルムを使用するという結果になってしまった。編集する段階でカメラのサイズよりもフィルムの種類の違いの方がはるかに写真の仕上がりに影響が大きいことに驚いた。カメラも進歩しているが、フィルムの方も負けずに年々改善されているということだろう。

●多々のカメラ、フィルムを使用してきたが、最終的にはモノクロームの撮影には35ミリカメラボディ１台、レンズ24ミリ、60ミリ、100ミリ、180ミリの4本、フィルムはテクニカルパン一種類と落ち着いたようだ。必要最小限の器材を徹底的に使いこなし、それを十分に生かすという私が前から主張している方法だ。

フィルム…	ネオパンF
	さくら赤外
	プラスX
	イルフォードパンF
	テクニカルパン
カメラ……	6×6型＝ハッセルブラードM型
	35ミリ＝ニコンF、ライカR3
レンズ……	6×6型＝プラナー80㎜ F2.8
	ゾナー250㎜ F5.6
	35ミリ＝ニッコール24㎜ F2.8
	ニッコール50㎜ F2
	ニッコール135㎜ F3.5
	エルマリート24㎜ F2.8
	マクロエルマリート60㎜ F2.8
	マクロエルマリート100㎜ F4
	エルマリート180㎜ F4

PHOTOGRAPHY NOTE

◉ Even though I love her, I do not love her enough. Even though I am climbing here, I am not climbing her. Even though I am photographing her, I can not capture her. These are the strong sentiments I have of Hodaka in my mountains climbing excursions. Her features and rugged jags and crevasses transform with the seasons, climate and time.

◉ Because I thought a small 35 mm camera would be useful in dealing with mountains, over 90% of the photographs compiled in this book were taken by the one. In the result, various cameras and films were used over a long period of twenty years. During editing I was surprised to find that the difference in the type of film had a clear effect on the finish of the photographs rather than the size of the camera. Although cameras have gotten better, yearly improvements in films have been made, as well. Various cameras and films have been employed and the most recent monochromes were taken with a 35 mm camera body and four types of lens 24 mm, 60 mm, 100 mm and 180 mm. The type of film was technical-pan which gave its calming effect. I adhere to using the minimal necessary supply and equipment. As I have advocated before it is my method to make the most use out of them.

あとがき

　ここに集められた作品は1966年から1986年にかけて撮影されたものである。　これは即ち私が写真を始めてから今日までということになり、実に20年間モノクロームによる穂高の写真にこだわり続けてきたことになる。

　しかし、初期の作品と最近撮影したものと並べても、フィルムなどテクニック上の違いはあるものの、作品そのものの違和感は感じられなかった。これはテーマをしぼり計画的に撮影してきて狙いが決まっていたからに違いない。

　この狙いとは、穂高を山の象徴と考え、すべての山が共通して持っている高さ、大きさ、深さ、厳しさ、険しさ、清さ、豊かさ、美しさといったものを、私なりに見つめ写真を通して追求してきたことである。

　一つのものにのめり込み、集中しだすとほかが見えなくなるという私の性格から、山登りは常に私に暗い影を落としていた。しかし、自分の仕事と山とを結びつけることによって、自分の人生が開かれてきた。そして山に登るという行動から自然とふれあう喜びを知り、しだいに自然を見る私の眼が広がりを持ってきた。

　そして最近、自然への興味が山だけではなく広い世界に向いてくると、私の写真は山岳写真といわれるところから少しずつ遠ざかっていく傾向にある。

　この写真集は、再びあれほど新鮮な感動を持って純粋に山に集中できるとは考えられない今、自分の山岳写真をまとめたものである。

　この20年間に非常に多くの方々のお世話になり助けていただいた。その方々一人ひとりに心からなる感謝の気持を伝えたい。

　とくにいつも変わらず私の心の支えであった田淵行男先生、常に親身になってバックアップして下さった穂高岳山荘の今田英雄氏、嘉門次小屋の上条輝夫氏の御好意は忘れることができません。山行をともにした青柳淳氏、神憲明氏、田代宏君をはじめとした多くの山の先輩、友人にはほんとうに長い間お世話になりました。

　また、この写真集の出版にあたって、巻頭に井上靖先生の序文をいただいたことは望外の喜びでした。

　デザインの鈴木一誌氏、そして、この本の企画・編集を担当して下さり、私の我がままをきいて下さったグラフィック社の赤平覚三氏に謹んでお礼を申し上げます。

　最後になってしまいましたが、私の写真をプリントして下さった川名信也氏には、この写真集は二人の共著であると言っても過言ではないような御苦労をおかけしました。

　ほんとうにありがとうございました。

冬の浅間山麓にて　1986年2月21日

水越武

AFTERWORD

The compiled works here, which my first photographs to my most recent ones, were taken from 1966 to 1986. Thus, I have been faithfully taking monochrome photographs of Hodaka for the last twenty years.

Although there were differences in the type of film and technique used when I put my earlier work side by side with my most recent ones, I did not sense a feeling of incompatibility. That is because I have narrowed down my theme and deliberately set my aim in the photographing of them. In this aim Hodaka could be considered the symbol of mountains. By the way of photographs as seen through my eyes I have pursued a commonness found in all mountains the height, size, depth, harshness, ruggedness, nobleness, richness and beauty.

Because it was my character to become completely engrossed in one thing so much that I was blind to all, mountain climbing eclipsed everything else. However, due to mountains being related to my work it opend up my life. I have come to know the splendors of nature touching it through my mountain climbing activities which has gradually expanded my perspective of nature. Recently, as my interest in nature has moved beyond mountains and spreaded to other things throughout the world, my photographs have begun to shift little by little from so-called mountain landscapes. This collection was compiled of photographs I took myself which I do not think I could ever do again with the same raw sensitivity and pure concentration on mountains.

Over these last twenty years I have received aid and encouragement from many various people and I would like to thank them from the bottom of my heart. In particular, I will never forget Mr. Yukio Tabuchi for his spiritual encouragement he always gave me, Hideo Imada of Hodaka-Dake Mountain Resort who warmheartedly gave me support and Teruo Kamijo of Kamonji Cottage who showed me kindness. I would like to also express my sincere appreciation to Jun Aoyagi, Noriaki Jin, and Hiroshi Tashiro and all my many fellow mountain climbing companions.

Concerning the publication of this photo collection, I was extremely honored to have the pleasant surprise of the renown writer Yasushi Inoue write the foreword. I would also like to extend my gratitude to Hitoshi Suzuki for design and Kakuzo Akahira of Graphic-sha Publishing Co., who was in charge with the planning and editing of this book as well as accepted my requests. Lastly, I would like to thank Shinya Kawana who did a marvelous job on printing my pictures and it would not be an exaggeration to say that this photo collection was the work of two of us. Thank you very much for all your hard work.

At the foot of Asama **February 21, 1986**
Takeshi Mizukoshi

水越武略歴

◉1938年愛知県に生まれる。
主に山岳, 自然写真を撮って現在に至る。
マッキンレーを始めカラコルム, ヒマラヤ, 中国の山に多数遠征。
◉現在, 日本写真家協会会員。
近年, プラハ, アムステルダムで個展を開催。
◉著書に,
《山の輪舞》
《日本アルプスの花》他多数。
◉**現住所:**
長野県北佐久郡御代田町草越1190-2

About
TAKESHI MIZUKOSHI

◉Born in 1938 in Aichi Prefecture.
Specializes in photographs of mountains and nature.
Has made numerous trips to Mt. McKinley,
the Karakorum, the Himalayas,
and the mountain ranges of China.
Currently a member of
the Japan Photographers' Association.
Recently exhibited at one-man shows in Prague and Amsterdam.
◉Has published a number of books
including *Dance of the Mountains* and
Flowers of the Japan Alps.

◉**Address:**
1190-2 Kusagoe, Miyotamachi Kita Saku Gun,
Nagano389-02, Japan

The Hodaka
Radiance and Wind in the Japan Alps
photographed by
Takeshi Mizukoshi

穂高
光と風
水越武写真集
1986年6月25日 初版第1刷発行

2,900円 | 定価
水越武© | 著者
久世利郎 | 発行者
凸版印刷株式会社 | 印刷所
凸版印刷株式会社 | 製本所
株式会社プロスタディオ | 写植
株式会社グラフィック社 | 発行所
〒102 東京都千代田区九段北1-9-12
電話03・263・4318 振替・東京3-114345
落丁・乱丁本はお取替え致します。
ISBN4-7661-0381-5 C0072 ¥2900E